THE STORY OF
BEING
YOU

THE STORY OF
BEING YOU

SANJAY DUA

Worldwide Published by

Pendown Press

PENDOWN PRESS LLP

An ISO 9001 & ISO 14001 Certified Co.,

Regd. Office: 3767A, Kanhaiya Nagar,

Tri Nagar, Delhi-110035

Ph.: 8130886000, 9650072927

E-mail: info@pendownpress.com

Branch Office: 1A/2A, 20, Hari Sadan, Ansari Road,

Daryaganj, New Delhi-110002

Ph.: 011-45794768

Website: PendownPress.com

Edition: 2025

ISBN: 978-93-6338-651-8

Layout and Cover Designed by Pendown Graphics Team
Printed and Bound in India by Thomson Press India Ltd.

AUTHOR'S NOTE 

I have always been a keen observer of human emotions, thoughts, and behaviours. Since childhood, I found myself drawn to the complexities of the human mind - how people react to situations, how they process emotions, and, most importantly, how they cope with failure.

Through my observations and experiences, I realized that failure is one of the most misunderstood aspects of life. Too often, people see it as the end rather than a phase, a lesson, or even an opportunity. I have met many who lost hope, who felt stuck in the darkness of disappointment, unable to see a way forward.

This book is my attempt to reach those who have struggled with failure - to let them know they are not alone, and that there is always hope. Every story in this book carries a message, a reminder that emotions, no matter how overwhelming, can be understood, embraced, and transformed.

I hope that as you read these stories, you find a reflection of your own journey within them. And more than anything, I hope they serve as a reminder that failure is not the opposite of success; it is a part of it.

Transformationally Yours,

Sanjay Dua

A Canvas of Stories to Transform Lives

PART I

GRATITUDE, KINDNESS, AND RELATIONSHIPS

1

A DEBT OF KINDNESS

"In a world where you can be anything, be KIND!"

- Anonymous

For every kid who grew up in the '90s, a ₹5 Mango Frooti in a Tetra pack was more than just a drink-it was a summer ritual, a source of pure joy. As the temperatures soared, the small shop in our neighbourhood became the hotspot. The shopkeeper, one of the few selling Frooti, practically ruled the season. Demand was so high that we often stood in long queues, sometimes waiting 15–20 minutes just to get our hands on one.

One scorching afternoon, as we stood in line, something caught our attention. A boy, slightly older than us, casually walked up to the shopkeeper without adhering to the queue, strangely, the shopkeeper didn't object and instead handed him two Frootis, and the boy left without paying. This happened almost every day for a week before some of my friends finally confronted the shopkeeper.

"We've been waiting so long, yet you never ask him to stand in line. And you don't even take money from him. Why?" one of them asked, clearly frustrated.

The shopkeeper paused as if lost in thought. Then, with a sigh, he said, "It's a long story."

At our insistence, he finally shared it. The boy's father had once been a successful businessman, and the shopkeeper had worked under him. During those years, he learned everything about

running a business from this man. However, an unfortunate event led to the businessman's downfall, leaving his family struggling to meet even basic needs.

"When I heard about their situation," the shopkeeper continued, "I knew I had to do something. His father never asked for help-never even hinted at it. But I wanted to give back in whatever small way I could. He once took care of me and guided me when I was a nobody. Now, life has given me a chance to return the favour. Offering his kids these sweet drinks is my way of showing gratitude."

That day, we walked away not just with our Frootis but with a lesson that would stay with us for life.

> In life, kindness is often repaid in ways we don't expect.
>
> The hands that lift us today may be the ones that need lifting tomorrow. Life is a cycle, and if we pay attention, it always gives us a chance to return what we once received.

2

THE GIVER

*"A man there was, and they called him mad;
the more he gave, the more he had."*

- John Bunyan

Ah, the fond aroma of memories! Kaveri-for those from Ranchi, the name brings up the feeling of a homely place with delicious food. Especially its famous Paneer Chili that is sure to have a special place in your heart (and taste buds).

At the bank where our mom worked, the twice-a-year ritual during the bank's closing time was also the time for a full-blown corporate celebration. While most of the bank staff dined in the office, our mom, being the thoughtful soul she is, brought the feast home for me and my sister. It became a yearly highlight, an event eagerly awaited by the whole family.

The joy on our faces, as we relished those rare, delicious meals from Kaveri, became the priceless reward for our mom's effort. It's a beautiful example of the essence of relationships-about giving, creating moments, and savouring the simple pleasures that brighten our lives.

Who knew that a humble food packet could hold so much warmth and love?

The sheer joy in our faces while having that meal used to make my mother so happy. The pleasure derived from uplifting others moods was something she always lived for, and it was quite evident in her smiles, as we enjoyed the meal.

Indulge in the joy of giving, and see the extent of satisfaction you derive from it. Such happiness is life-changing.

3

GRATITUDE

"Gratitude will shift you to a higher frequency,
and you will attract much better things."

– Rhonda Byrne

The power of gratitude is so underrated. It's not always easy to think that way, counting your blessings and all that has brought you to where you are now standing.

My mother used to get Rs. 800 as a monthly salary in the year 1987 and used to take care of all our necessities. And still, she used to keep 10% of that amount aside (which she categorises as 'Daswant') to help people in need and for any other noble, charitable cause. She continues to do the same today, even post-retirement.

She always says you should be grateful irrespective of whether you get 800 or 800 lacs of Rupees. The power of gratitude is so infectious.

Don't wait for things to be perfect before you feel grateful. In fact, it is the other way around, the more grateful you are for wherever you are right now, the better your life will get.

Try your hand to cultivate an "attitude of gratitude".
It will take you a long way, I promise!

4

THE BEST MEDICINE

*"Too often we underestimate the power of a touch, a smile,
a kind word, a listening ear, an honest compliment,
or the smallest act of caring, all of which have
the potential to turn a life around."*
– Leo Buscaglia

Back in school days, one of our classmates had been absent from classes for long. Soon, we learned that he was ill and we went to his place to meet him. Laid on his bed, he was very low on energy, and not able to eat or even talk. His mother told us that he had been dull and down for days.

Shocked to see him in this condition, we hugged and cuddled him, and started sharing childhood memories with him. After a while, a slight smile started appearing on his face. The two hours we spent at his place helped him feel better, and when we left his place he had a big smile on his face. A complete change from the boy who we saw on arrival! After a day, he even started coming to school! On learning that he was healing so quickly, and was much better, we were delighted but surprised.

Later, his mother shared with us, that he was expecting his friends to come and meet him. He had silently wished and prayed that his friends would be concerned about his well-being and health. Miraculously, we actually visited him!

7

This is the balance of life for you. As you build a relationship, there is a give and take that keeps the relationship healthy. The other individual in the relationship expects and wishes for significant value from your side. When you make them feel like someone special, a 'hero', someone who matters, they feel seen, heard, and valued and their inner frustrations naturally fade away.

Someone once asked, "What is the best medicine?", to which the other person replied, "Love". When asked again, "What if love is not sufficient?", the reply came immediately, "Then increase the dose of love".

> Values like respect and significance are often the tools to heal all your problems and worries in life.

5

THE GIFT OF TIME

*"The greatest gift you can give someone is your time.
Because when you give your time, you are giving a portion
of your life that you will never get back."*
— Anonymous

Someone once asked, "What is the best gift one can give to someone?". Hearing this, people gave different answers such as cash, jewellery, electronic gadgets, books, and so on.

With so many different answers, finally, the discussion concluded with the realization, that all these things follow an up-down pattern, where they rise and fall with each passing day. If you make an investment today, it will most likely give you more returns tomorrow, or in rare unfortunate cases it might go down. If you buy a gadget, a newer model will come out soon.

However, there is one thing that only decreases with time-our time itself. The time you have on this planet is limited.

However, besides all these things, time is the only thing that solely follows a declining pattern and decreases with time-your time itself! The time you have on this planet is limited. Once a moment is gone, it never comes back. That's why the most valuable gift you can give someone is your time.

If you devote and allot some of your time to spend with someone, it is the best way of honoring them...

So, the next time you are confused about what to gift someone, try this - sit with them, talk to them, listen to them. Give them your undivided attention. Because nothing in the world is more precious than the time you spend with the people you care about. Spend quality time with them, because there cannot be a more perfect gift than that.

❖ ❖ ❖ ❖

6

FORGIVE AND FORGET

"Without forgiveness, life is governed by an endless cycle of resentment and retaliation."
– Roberto Assagioli

Childhood is filled with so many little, but vital incidents that silently teach us values like forgiveness. When we were young, we would often have petty differences with our friends. After each fight, we would run to our parents and complain about it. Both sets of parents would then come together and make us hug each other, saying, "Chalo ab bhool jao, aur khelo." "Forgive and forget and go and play"

This little statement and forgiveness ritual would erase all the confusion between friends and we would return to playing and enjoying together.

However, once childhood passes away, the scenario shifts completely. When those same set of friends grow up into mature individuals, they no longer fall back on the support of their parents to help them forgive each other. So what happens? Now when arguments or differences come up, they are not resolved effortlessly with hugs. Ultimately, they end up retaining those harsh feelings inside themselves and are unable to forgive, forget, and move on.

Sometimes, people may misunderstand you, argue with you, or say things that hurt you. These moments can affect you, even if

you don't realize it. All these things silently cause you harm. The real problem is when you keep thinking about them. Each time you replay those negative moments in your mind, they hurt you all over again and they affect your mental health.

> Therefore, forgiveness is essential not just for maintaining better relationships but for your well-being as well. Science is a witness to the fact that forgiveness improves your mental health. It helps you fight depression and anxiety. It is not just important because it helps you forgive someone, but helps you accept yourself for who you are.

7

TRUE SUPPORTERS

"True supporters aren't the ones who always cheer you on, but the ones who challenge you to be better—even when it's uncomfortable."
– Sanjay Dua

When I studied in the eighth grade, I loved my Sanskrit teacher wholeheartedly. I would study very well during his classes and would answer most of the questions he asked the students. He too supported and complimented me for my performance. Thus, he became my favourite in school.

One fine day, he scolded and rebuked me for being naughty in class. This made me feel extremely bad and unhappy, and I decided that he was not my 'favourite' teacher anymore. The embarrassment of being scolded by him in front of all my friends shook me badly.

It was simple. I kept adoring him until he complimented me in class. But as soon as he scolded me and told me something that was meant for my own good, but in front of the entire class, I felt he was not my true supporter.

Little did I understand then that your real supporters are those who truly care for your growth and development in every situation. No matter if their thoughts don't align with yours, they will always put you on priority, and care for your good. They might give you a reality check in ways that you find harsh, but remember that it is always intended for your good.

All you need is that pair of spectacles tinted with wisdom and discernment to help you distinguish your true supporters from the rest of the world.

So, choose those people who might sometimes place you in difficult, uncomfortable situations, but only for your betterment, and to guide you to the right path.

8

LOVE

"The purest form of love is the kind that expects nothing, asks for nothing, and gives everything."
– Sanjay Dua

There is this heartwarming story of a man who had been unemployed for some days. He and his family were going through tough times, and for three long days, they had nothing to eat. Hunger had become their constant companion, making life very difficult.

Then, on the 4th day, things started to look a little brighter. The man managed to earn a very small amount of money. With that small amount, he rushed to buy food for his family. The sight of food brought immense joy and relief to their faces. They were finally going to have a meal after days of going hungry.

But just as they began to eat and savour the food, there was a knock on their door. The man got up to answer it and found a group of people standing there, asking for help. These people were in a desperate situation; they hadn't had a meal in the past seven days.

Now, here's where the story takes an inspiring turn.

Despite his own hunger and the fact that his family had only just started to eat, this kind-hearted man didn't hesitate. He took his own food and shared as much as he could with the hungry strangers at his door.

What he did that day wasn't merely help; it was an act of pure selflessness and love. Even though he was already struggling to feed his family, he didn't think twice about helping others in need.

> This, my friend, is the true definition of love - the kind
> of love that goes beyond words and self-interest,
> showing compassion and care for others,
> even in the midst of one's own challenges.

PART II

EMOTIONAL INTELLIGENCE AND SELF-DISCOVERY

9

EMOTIONAL WELLBEING

*"Some of us think holding on makes us strong
but sometimes it is letting go."*
– Herman Hesse

Think about a pond or a puddle. When water stays in one place for too long, mosquitoes start to gather. This isn't just bad for you-it's bad for nature too. However, wherever water is flowing and not stagnant, it does not attract mosquitoes or dirt. This is the law of nature.

Now, think about your mind. Every day, thousands of thoughts and emotions come and go. That's completely normal. The real problem starts when you hold onto certain thoughts for too long, just like the still water attracts mosquitoes these thoughts begin to mess with your peace of mind. This can cause problems for your mental well-being.

So, when a thought or feeling enters your mind, don't stress. Let it come and go, like water flowing in a stream. If you hold onto it too long, it can disturb your peace. The key is to let things flow!

10

YOUR EMOTIONAL THERMOSTAT

"When our emotional health is in a bad state, so is our level of self-esteem. We have to slow down and deal with what is troubling us so that we can enjoy the simple joy of being happy and at peace with ourselves."
– Jess C. Scott

Imagine it's getting colder as winter approaches. You have a small device in your hand, like a temperature control knob on a fan. If you're feeling chilly, you can turn the knob down to make it warmer, and if you're feeling hot, you turn it up to cool down. This device helps you adjust to the changing environment.

Now, think about the feelings and emotions bubbling up inside you. Some feelings are light, like a gentle breeze, while others can be strong, like a gust of wind.

If you had a way to control your emotions, just like adjusting the fan, life would be easier.

Managing your emotions is not about pushing them away; it's about handling them in the right way. It's like finding the perfect setting on the knob. But to do that, you first need to understand your emotions and then figure out how to handle them. It's about acknowledging, accepting, and then responding to them.

As children grow up, they experience lots of emotions, just like the changing weather. It's important for them to learn whom to share their feelings with, how to manage them, and how to regulate them, just like adjusting that fan knob to stay comfortable.

11

SELF-ACCEPTANCE

> *"Because true belonging only happens when we present our*
> *authentic, imperfect selves to the world, our*
> *sense of belonging can never be greater than*
> *our level of self-acceptance."*
> **– Brené Brown**

In the backdrop of our lives stood a 500-square-foot house, a space that served as the living room, dining area, and bedroom. Our home was quite compact, and thus, I would constantly wonder how to invite my friends over to this little house of mine. Even when my friends would come over for a considerable time for enjoyable lengthy conversations, I would keep them sitting outdoors, never inviting them to step inside the house.

Then, on a particular day, my mother commented on this pattern. She inquired why I avoided bringing my friends inside. I gave her a silly excuse that made no sense at all, telling her that my friends departed quickly, leaving the conversation incomplete, there was never enough time to invite them in.

However, with her comment and inquiry, my mother conveyed a crucial lesson that day. She taught me the necessity of embracing whatever circumstances life had given us. Be it our present possessions or future acquisitions, her words resonated-their acceptance was important.

She pointed out that unless I could accept myself and my reality, any show I would put up in front of others would be hollow, quite contrary to my actual world. To win genuine acceptance from others, it was essential to first embrace my own truth. This insight, profound in its simplicity, struck a chord. The act of acknowledging the reality of our situation, she emphasised, helped us to begin our self-improvement and personal growth.

In conclusion, her lesson showed me a path of authenticity. It highlighted that progress starts with self-acceptance-the foundation upon which personal achievement is constructed.

12

IT'S ALL ABOUT PERSPECTIVE!

"Empathy begins with understanding life from another person's perspective. Nobody has an objective experience of reality. It's all through our own individual prisms."
– Sterling K. Brown

One time, my family and I were invited to a relative's house for dinner. They had prepared a lavish spread of various dishes, and it was a bit overwhelming. Some of the dishes on the table were not to my liking, while there were a few sweet treats that I really craved.

In my attempt to be polite and not offend our hosts, I decided to start with the dishes I didn't like. I thought I would eat the dishes I loved later, once I had cleared the ones I didn't enjoy.

Naturally, I acted like I was enjoying them, even though I knew they didn't match my food choices. However, an interesting thing happened. My relative, observing that I was enjoying the dishes I disliked, assumed that those were my favourites and generously served me more of those dishes.

This situation reflects something we often encounter in our lives. You see, I had one perspective; I was trying to be polite by eating the dishes I didn't like. But my relative had a different perspective

and thought I genuinely liked those dishes, so he wanted to make me happy by offering more.

The point here is about the acceptance of different viewpoints. It's natural for people to have varying perspectives based on their experiences and backgrounds. We tend to interpret situations through the lens of our own past, and what we think might not always align with what others believe. Ultimately, we get stuck in our own web of assumptions.

It's essential to remember that our way of seeing things is not the only way, and sometimes, what others think or feel also matters. By being open to different viewpoints, we can build better understanding and connections with the people around us. It's a reminder that the world is full of diverse perspectives, and that's what makes it interesting and rich.

13

MIND SWEEP

Sweeping is a regular routine done at every home. It ensures your interiors are neat and tidy, removing any dust that settles down. A clean house makes you feel good and uplifts your mood as well. Right?

But wait, what if I told you that you can do a mind sweep just like a house sweep- so, what is a mind sweep?

Well, just like your home, your mind too needs some occasional sweeping! It calms you from within and makes you feel lighter on the inside.

How exactly do you sweep your mind?

Take a piece of paper. Note down every thought that comes to your mind. Make a quick list of the tasks you are yet to do during the day, any thoughts that you came across, and any other ideas that you feel like writing down. It could be undesirable comments you heard from someone or even a compliment you received from a friend.

Practise this for 10 minutes straight.

Once you are done, you will realise that you have emptied your mind and it feels light. This is because you transferred all your thoughts that clogged your mind, onto the piece of paper.

Now, draw some blocks on the paper and jot down every pending task in a specific block, according to the slot you plan to do it in. Then, complete all your work according to the assigned block, one by one.

> 99 percent of your problems vanish away just when you write them down. Journaling as a habit helps you clean your mind, and focus on your work better.
> It makes you more efficient, productive, and peaceful while distancing you from all clumsiness and clutter.
>
> So, the next time, make sure you do a mind sweep, along with your house sweep!

14

THE GLOW

"There is no higher religion than human service.
To work for the common good is the greatest creed."
— Woodrow Wilson

Childhood memories often carry profound lessons, and this tale of candle-lit competitions is one of them. The kids would compete to see whose candle flame would last the longest. What began as a friendly competition took a turn when parents proposed a change in the game. Instead of waiting for each other's lights to extinguish first, the focus shifted to keeping every house illuminated.

The new game became a team effort, with kids going from house to house, ensuring that every candle stayed aglow.

The lesson learned during those late-night candle-lighting sessions was simple yet powerful-while lighting up one house is good; the true magic lies in illuminating every house.

In a world where the search for personal success often takes centre stage, this childhood experience teaches a timeless truth. Beyond the desire for more material possessions, the real victory is in bringing light to someone else's life.

Just as a fully lit lane during Diwali holds a special charm, spreading happiness involves not just brightening our own homes but helping others light up theirs too. It's a reminder that the collective glow is the key to creating something truly special.

15

IMPRESSIONS Vs AUTHENTICITY

"Authenticity means erasing the gap between what you firmly believe inside and what you reveal to the outside world."
– *Adam Grant*

As we were growing up, a familiar philosophy or instruction echoed through our homes, "Behave well", and this instruction and expectation were specially strengthened when guests were around or during outings to the market.

Thus, this idea that we should show the best version of ourselves in the presence of non-family members, became deeply ingrained in us. Resultantly, the desire to leave a positive impression on others was born-a desire to hear them say, "Wow, they're so well-behaved."

As time went by, this desire to impress took a deeper and more complex form known as **FOPO, or the fear of other people's opinions.**

It became a serious concern, causing us to worry about what others might think of us and how our lives should be shaped.

This worry resulted in a gradual separation between our authentic selves and the carefully crafted image we wished

to show the world. The larger this gap became, the more we found ourselves in a state of confusion and stress.

Every individual has a unique journey to navigate. Instead of constantly striving to live up to the expectations of others, we should focus on living authentically.

> Live your life for yourself, embracing authenticity and staying true to your identity. Let the world see and appreciate the real you, free from the weight of constant comparison and the fear of judgment.

16

BOREDOM

"Boredom has an important function because pushing through it can unleash creativity."
– Amy Dickinson

Some time back, I was traveling on a train with my family. My son suddenly said, "Papa, I am getting bored."

Boredom is a term that we hear seldom in today's advanced world. You would rarely hear someone admit that they are getting bored nowadays. The reason? There is so much that technology has blessed us with. The moment people move towards boredom, they immediately start scrolling their phones, checking their social media notifications, or deriving entertainment from any source.

Individuals today are so addicted to entertainment, that the human brain is equipped with the 'doing' aspect all through the day and night. There is so much rush and stress, that the brain doesn't get to remain idle for even a moment. Ultimately, it has no time to even get bored! And even if it does, we don't allow it to remain bored, and jump on to 'doing' something.

Research by several neuroscientists says that boredom actually enhances one's creativity. When you get bored, your brain cells get time for relaxation, which is when your creativity builds. In fact, boredom even helps you strengthen social connections and take a dive into an insightful mind.

So, the next time you get bored, enjoy the process of boredom too! Allow yourself to experience boredom, rather than immediately switching to some other tasks. Don't just rush into doing something to relieve boredom. Let your brain relax, take life slow, rejuvenate, and spark your creativity!

17

UNIQUENESS

"Comparison is an act of violence against the self!"
— Iyanla Vanzant

There is an interesting fable about a playground filled with grass everywhere. One fine day, someone came to the playground and placed a plant near the grass. On seeing this, the grass started wondering who the plant was.

In a few days, the plant grew bigger in size. The grass continued pondering over who it was, and the fact that people sat under its shade. The grass began comparing itself to the plant and felt it was still the same height as it was some time back, but the plant that had suddenly entered the playground recently had grown to quite an extent.

One evening, a dreadful storm shattered the surroundings. The plant too gave way, falling down to the ground with a thud. This made the grass realise the power of foundation and capability, which the plant lacked. It grew up quickly but didn't have as much capability to withstand the pressures of the storm. On the contrary, the grass being firmly grounded had such internal strength that even if it didn't grow much, it could win over the challenges of the storm.

This tale has a lesson for all of us.

Each one of us has something unique within us. Some
of us might be able to give shade just like the plant,
while some might be internally strong like the grass.
But the day we start comparing ourselves to others, just
like the grass did, we will fail to be our true selves. Once
you identify who you truly are, there will be no need for
you to turn to others and compare yourself with them.

PART III

OVERCOMING CHALLENGES AND RESILIENCE

18

HOPE

Once upon a time, there was a group of boys who decided to go on a hiking trip in the woods. As they went deeper into the forest, the path became steeper and more challenging. One of the boys found it tough to climb. He felt exhausted and thought he wouldn't be able to keep up with his friends.

Feeling discouraged, the boy decided to give up and sat down on a large rock, thinking he couldn't go any further. But his friends didn't want to leave him behind. They gathered around and offered words of encouragement. "You can do it, friend! Just take one step at a time, and we'll be with you all the way."

With the support of his friends and their encouraging words, he gathered the strength to continue. Slowly but steadily, he took one step at a time. His friends walked alongside him, motivating him to keep going.

After about half an hour, something amazing happened. The group realised that the boy had covered a significant distance, and he was no longer the one left behind. He had conquered the challenging path, and they had all completed their trek successfully.

This story teaches us an important lesson. Sometimes, we face difficult challenges in life, and we may doubt our abilities. We

might need some encouragement, skills, and competencies to achieve our goals, but above all, we need hope.

This is also illustrated beautifully by another story-

Once upon a time, there were numerous antique pieces kept inside a museum. One of them was a mirror, which people crowded around, enjoying themselves looking at their reflections in the glass.

One day, the mirror broke into pieces. The same mirror that was adored by visitors some time back, was now considered a bad omen on breaking apart. Kids were told not to move around the mirror fearing they would hurt themselves.

However, one little girl came forward with silver and golden tape. She started covering the cracks on the mirror with the tape. Soon, a few kids started helping her in the process and the mirror was once again ready after two hours.

The mirror, when broken into pieces, did not have anyone around it. But those kids became the support it needed to put itself back together.

We live through so many ups and downs in life. When you feel low and frustrated, there is nothing to worry about. **Instead, keep your hopes high**. The Universe's energy shall come and lift you up, be it in any form. Keep your eyes and ears open. Who knows, when that support system will come and rebuild you into a better and newer version of yourself?

> With hope and the support of friends or loved ones, we can overcome obstacles that initially seemed impossible to win over. It reminds us that a little encouragement can go a long way in helping us reach our aspirations.

19

EMOTIONAL FREEDOM

"True freedom isn't about winning battles or seeking
revenge–it's about rising above anger, ego,
and resentment.
The strongest hearts are the ones that choose
peace over punishment."
– Sanjay Dua

My childhood seems to have had its fair share of aggressive moments, with revenge being the go-to response. Yet, my mother, in all her simplicity, never let those negative vibes touch her. The way she handled difficulties and extended help to those who wronged her is a lesson in itself.

Imagine facing someone who has left no stone unturned to bring chaos into your life. The natural instinct would be to take revenge, to make them taste a bit of their own medicine. But no, my mother chose to extend a helping hand, a gesture that left them in awe and confusion.

Arguing with her felt like a debate; while I fought for justice, she calmly stood for freedom from anger, revenge, and ego.

In her calm and collected aura, she painted a vivid
picture of true freedom - one that goes
beyond negative emotions.

My childhood lessons taught me the importance of resilience
and an understanding of what it truly
means to be free within.

And the definition of freedom was set
straight once and forever.

20

REVENGE

"The best revenge is to be unlike him who performed the injury."
– Marcus Aurelius

When we were kids and played outside with our friends, we often got bitten by mosquitoes. And what did we do? We would try to swat those mosquitoes because we felt like they bit us, so we had to get back at them. As we grew up, this way of thinking stuck with us.

In today's world, if someone hurts or offends you, the first thought that often crosses your mind is, "I'll do the same to them. I'll show them why they shouldn't have done that to me." It's like a 'tit for tat' reaction, where you feel the need to prove that you can hurt someone, just like they hurt you.

But the thing is, this kind of thinking can turn you into someone you're not in real life. It's like saying, "Scorpions sting, so I'll sting back." But just because scorpions sting doesn't mean that you have to be like them, maybe you are a butterfly or a bird that chooses to rise higher and fly above these petty thoughts. Stay true to who you really are, and don't let negative actions define you.

21

GROWING UP IS OVERRATED

*"That's the real trouble with the world,
too many people grow up."*
– Walt Disney

As parents, we often tell our children to grow up, act their age, and follow certain expectations. We set these markers not just when they are kids but throughout their lives - when they grow up, get married, reach middle age, and even in their old age. We constantly measure them and expect them to take on certain responsibilities.

Sometimes, as adults, we become so focused on these responsibilities that we forget to enjoy the present moment. Some of us forget to enjoy our school and college days, and before we know it, we reach a point in life where we miss those times.

Instead of always telling our children to hurry and grow up, maybe we should encourage them to savour the present moments of their lives. If they make the most of today, their future will take care of itself.

22

UPS AND DOWNS

If you are aiming at the top, consistency is the name of the game."
– Olawale Daniel

Snakes and Ladders is a game that we are all so deeply connected with. It's an integral part of our childhoods. It consists of a dice, that is thrown with every chance. As you hop onto a big ladder, you climb to the top. But the next moment, a snake bites you and you fall down once again to the bottom.

Even with all these ups and downs, the most special part about this game is that no matter how much you fall, you continue to play your part. You never stop throwing the dice at every chance. You keep playing in the hope that a ladder will again help you get to the top.

Life is filled with the same ups and downs. Some situations help you climb up toward success, while some bring you down, trying to weaken you. **But what you must remember in these times, is to be consistent.**

Even in the lowest moments that make you feel frustrated, you must not stop taking your baby steps. Who knows, the next chance might just take you to a ladder that will help you climb to the extreme top! Just like the game of Snakes and Ladders, life must go on.

23

HUSTLE AND GRIND

"If you take shortcuts you get cut short."
– Gary Busey

One of the biggest turning points that changed my approach was when I failed my Mathematics exam in the eighth grade. The subject never really appealed to me. Every time I studied for a Mathematics exam, my whole and sole motive was to secure passing marks. I would study selective topics and hope that enough questions to give me passing marks from those topics would be a part of the question paper.

After I failed that exam, I changed my approach to the subject. I stopped mugging up answers and instead began understanding and building up on my core concepts. Once I did this, my grades instantly began to rise. I even went ahead to pursue Mathematics Honours.

A realisation dawned upon me. As soon as I shifted my focus from just securing marks to actually learning my concepts well, I saw real change.

This happens so often in the bigger scenario of life. Sometimes, we chase small goals so religiously, that we end up taking shortcuts to achieve them. These shortcuts take us quickly towards the goal but often leave us only with temporary, short-lived success. Thus, our true development takes a back seat.

Instead of using shortcuts in life, try your hands at the
longer, tougher route, that involves hustle and grind.
If the Universe is not bringing you closer to achieving
your goals, take it as a sign that it wants you to work the
harder way. Rather than just ticking your checklist of
goals, enjoy the process that eventually leads you
to the pinnacle of success.

24

TEST OF LIFE

*"The ability to focus is a defining characteristic
of successful individuals."*
– Brian Tracy

There would be various subjects we studied back in school. After every class, the teacher who would come for the next one would ask us to rub the blackboard that had all the notes of the previous period's subject.

So, if we had a Mathematics class, the next teacher coming to teach Science would tell us to rub the Mathematics notes on the blackboard and open our Science textbooks to focus on that subject. She would specifically instruct us to pay attention only to that particular subject, not the previous one, and not even the next one. We would follow likewise, concentrating only on that topic, and would shift our focus to another subject as and when the next period would begin.

Since we religiously focussed on that one particular topic for the entire class, we would end up grasping it deeply. This would help us to write about it properly during examinations.

Compare this to your real-life time slots. We unknowingly devote separate time slots for all our activities during the day, be it work, exercise, studies, and so on. If you truly immerse yourself into what you are doing currently, leaving aside everything else, you will be able to do it better.

Your complete focus on your current activity would help you win the test of life. Make this habit a part of your routine and see what happens!

25

UNLEARN AND RELEARN

*"The first problem for all of us, men and women,
is not to learn, but to unlearn."*
– Gloria Steinem

Going for a morning walk on a fresh sunny day is so rejuvenating. In addition, the melodious chirping of birds that accompany you on your morning stroll feels like music to the ears.

One interesting thing to observe is that even though they keep chirping as you walk, they fly away out of fear as soon as they sense you are coming close. Their intuition prompts them to fly away whenever a car or a person comes in proximity, as they fear being hit by them. In fact, they go far away even when a group of children are playing and creating commotion.

When I was traveling some time back, I came across a couple of trained birds. As they perched with ease on my shoulders, they were devoid of fear. Even when I tried touching them, they didn't seem to get scared, nor did they fly away. In fact, one even sat on my head a while later.

I was amused by this incident. The same kind of birds that get scared even at the slightest of motion or sound, were now sitting so peacefully on my shoulders and head. Once they are trained, their self-belief, confidence, and connection with humans become strong.

When these birds can imbibe the sense of being brave so beautifully, why can't we? Just like they go through a period of training, our mind too needs to experience the process of unlearning and relearning. Unlearn the ideas that bind you unnecessarily, and prove to not be of much use. Similarly, pursue and follow the thoughts that keep you grounded and inspired, and push you towards a better version of yourself.

Part VI

Perspective and Mindset Shifts

26

LIFE IS HOW YOU VIEW IT

Once upon a time, two friends visited a museum. It had breathtaking furniture and a dazzling chandelier hanging from above. Both the friends had completely contrary views about it.

One of them said, "Wow! Look at that chandelier, it is beautiful." She started capturing the beauty of the chandelier on her camera, embracing its shine and sparkle.

On the other hand, her friend kept insisting on leaving the museum. She said, "This chandelier must be so heavy. Just imagine if it falls, it will take our lives." It was astonishing to find two people looking at the same object with such strikingly different perspectives.

This often happens in life. You will find a section of individuals who always look at situations in a positive, embracing manner. While there will always be another set of individuals who behave in a pessimistic way.

> It is not wrong to criticise something, but if you constantly keep looking at life with those negative perspectives, you cease to enjoy it. Just look at everything through a positive lens, and you will start spotting good even in the worst of times.

27

CARS AND OPPORTUNITIES

"If you believe it will work out, you will see opportunities.
If you believe it won't, you will see obstacles."
– Wayne Dyer

Spot the Car was a game we used to play during schooldays while travelling on the school bus. This is how it went; one person would spot cars of a particular colour on the road, while the other had to spot cars of another colour. The one who spotted the maximum number of cars in their colour would eventually win the game, to get a bar of Dairy Milk chocolate.

I clearly recall even now that I would keep complaining about the colour I was given. I would keep saying that cars of this colour don't even exist, so it is impossible to spot them. However, my friends would still insist I try spotting those cars.

After some time, I realised that cars of that colour really do exist, and I was able to spot three or four of them every single day. Did those cars exist even when I said they didn't? Of course, they always did exist. But when I wired my mind with all my focus only on cars of that particular design and colour, my eyes could identify them easily. The change was in my mindset, thinking, focus, and attention.

Similarly, life always presents you with so many opportunities in your surroundings. What you only need to do, is change your perspective. If you are fuelled with passion, and keep your eyes and ears open with utmost focus, you will find the opportunities meant for you.

28

SEASON AND REASON

"Some people cross our path momentarily, others walk beside us for a lifetime. The ones who truly matter aren't defined by time, but by the impact they leave on our hearts."
– Sanjay Dua

All through life, you meet various kinds of people at every stage. You meet some in school, some in college, and even in your professional world. Every individual comes into your life primarily for either a season or a reason.

The first kind of people who come for a season make short-lived connections with you. They usually meet you for a transactional purpose, or any sort of work, say a project. Once the work is done, you move on, and so do they.

The second type is those who come for a reason. They enter your world with such inspiration and interest and end up bringing a transformation in your life, be it big or small. They impact you in a way that never lets you forget them. I am sure you all have friends you remember and have stayed in touch with for years. You might not meet them often, but that bond never breaks apart. This is because, somewhere, they have fed meaning and purpose into your life, and have positively changed you.

> While ninety percent of your contacts come for a
> season, only a special ten percent are for a reason.
> All you need to do is identify those rare ten percent
> and keep them close to you, for they are the real gems.

29

THE SOLUTION IS 'YOU'

"You are the only problem you will ever have and you are the only solution. Change is inevitable, personal growth is always a personal decision."

– Bob Proctor

When we were kids, there was a popular belief about a bird called the Maina in India. We thought that if we saw two Maina birds together, it meant we were lucky, and if we saw only one, it meant we were unlucky, there was even a popular chant for this - **One for Sorrow; Two for Joy!** We took this idea very seriously when we were children. Every day before going to school, we would search for two Maina birds.

As we grew older, our friends would sometimes blame their bad days on seeing an unlucky face in the morning. We often tend to blame our problems on other people or things. We say, "I was perfect, and someone else caused the problem." We start trying to change the other person to solve our issues.

But the real solution doesn't lie outside; it's within you.

When you realise that your life isn't going the way you want, remember, you are responsible for it.

> No matter how hard you try to fix external problems, you won't find the result you seek until you address your inner issues. So, if you're looking for a solution, start by searching for the solution within yourself.

30

REAL JOY

"Happiness doesn't result from what we get,
but from what we give."
– Ben Carson

The rainy season came with unpredictable weather. While dark clouds filled the sky one moment, the sun shone in another. Amidst such a scenario, a friend's voice echoed, a reminder of an interrupted cricket game the evening before. We fancied ourselves as Master Blasters, each competing for the batting spotlight. However, a sudden shower of rain had cut short my friend's turn the previous day, and I kept teasing him about it.

Determined to rectify the unfinished game, he called out to me the next morning to continue where we had left off. The Sun and the Clouds again showed us similar weather patterns, like the previous day's scenario. Thus, my friend could not get his rightful turn to bat, yet again.

Little did I know then that my friend's upset face held a deeper reason-he and his family were moving away due to his father's job transfer. This news hit me hard the next day, leaving me thinking about all our shared memories and the fights we'd had over the past years.

A routine day turned into a revelation about the joy of giving. To lift his spirits before his departure, I decided to dedicate the entire day to making sure he had a proper turn at the bat.

As he left with a huge smile, a profound truth dawned on me-the happiness derived from making others happy brings a peace that goes far beyond the game's last ball.

31

BETS OR BONDS?

Going to the cafeteria during lunchtime is one of my fondest memories of school. There would be so many exciting dishes on the menu, chai, samosa, and whatnot!

Though we didn't have the privilege of going to the cafeteria every day, one of our friends did. He was very well off so he would treat us to the delicious snacks too. However, we didn't feel right about him treating us so often, and we requested him not to, so he stopped.

During those days, we would play a game of betting where the one who lost the bet would treat everyone else. Somehow the majority of the time, that same friend would lose the bet and ended up giving us all a treat.

It was only later that the realisation dawned upon us, that he would purposely lose his bets so that he could treat us. It was because he wanted to silently give us the treat which we had asked him not to. Though he was losing bets, he was winning our hearts!

We often try our best to win bets, or in more practical
terms, we want our words to be deemed right always.
But while doing that, we lose the value of our relationships.
Slowly, a time comes when people agree with what we say,
but in trying to prove ourselves right those relationships
lose their true essence. So, focus on the bonds you build,
not on the bets you lose!

32

THE EGO

— Jonny Kim

Once upon a time, there were two friends. While one couldn't see, the other couldn't walk. The one who couldn't see told the other to be friends with him. He said, "I can lift you onto my shoulders and carry you, while you can keep giving me directions so I know where to go. Since I can't see, your instructions can guide me properly. And since you can't walk, my shoulders will help you."

Both the friends collaborated and lived as a team, helping each other. However, after some time, their egos started dominating them. The blind friend thought, "If I stop carrying him on my shoulders, he will never be able to walk and his life will be ruined." The other friend thought of him in a similar way, that if he stopped guiding him, his life would be finished. With this, their friendship became weak and they fell apart.

One day God appeared before both friends and asked them to state one wish each, that they wanted to be granted. The blind friend said, "Make my friend blind just like me." The other friend also asked God to make his blind friend handicapped and unable to walk. Ultimately, both lost their two powers.

They could have easily asked for their vision and legs back, respectively. But they didn't, as their egos spoke loudly that time. When you let your ego take the front seat, you forget about your own wishes. Instead, you get engrossed in making life difficult for others.

> There are three kinds of people in relationships. First are those who don't want to harm anyone, they believe in 'Live and let live'. The second group consists of people that are selfish and want their good, but also don't want to cause harm to others. However, the last kind is just like these friends. While they don't care about themselves, they want to ensure others are not happy.
> So which kind do you belong to?

33

LIKES AND DISLIKES

"People are not good or bad-they are simply reflections of their own experiences.
The moment we let go of judgment, we open ourselves to understanding, growth, and a world of new perspectives."
– Sanjay Dua

We often tend to term some people as 'good' and some as 'bad' on the basis of whether we like or dislike them. But where does this liking or disliking come from?

Every time we do something in life, we silently seek validation from all those around us. If someone supports us in the process, matches and aligns with our thoughts, and likes us, we automatically call them 'good'. However, those who think contrary to us, have conflicting opinions, and debate views, we term them as 'bad'.

But think about this, everyone on this planet has a different story and perspective. If someone doesn't match your mindset, it probably means that they look at you and your story from a different perspective, which actually makes them unique.

This doesn't mean that the person is 'good' or 'bad', but rather, he/she comes with their own story and baggage of life. Thus, you both accept life at different face values.

These are approaches that often the formal education process doesn't teach you. Instead, your mind must be devoid of the clutter of likes and dislikes. Only then you will be able to understand every individual's perspective.

> If you treat everyone on an equal scale, you will realise you are learning something new from them in each situation, each moment. No one is good or bad, it is all about the lens through which you see them!

PART V

DECISION MAKING AND LIFE LESSONS

REACTIONS AND RESPONSES

– Brad Stulberg

There is an old popular story about a father who used to leave his two-year-old son at home with a protective mongoose while he went to work. One day, a dangerous snake entered their home, and the mongoose bravely fought and defeated it, but got hurt in the process because the snake's venom got into its body.

The mongoose, even though injured, waited outside for the father to return. When the father came back and saw the mongoose covered in blood, he wrongly thought that the mongoose had harmed his child. Without knowing the whole story, the father acted on impulse and killed the mongoose with a stone. Inside the house, the child was safe, and the dead snake lay in a corner. The father regretted his quick judgment.

This story reminds us that our quick thoughts and actions can shape our lives. Sometimes, we react without thinking, and those reactions can either make our lives better or worse. It's important to pause and think before reacting or making big decisions. This pause can change how we see things and how we approach life.

So, we have a choice - to react quickly and impulsively
or to take a moment to think and respond wisely.
By choosing to pause and think, we can change
the story of our lives for the better.

35

DECISION AND DILEMMA

"I have learned that as long as I hold fast to my beliefs and values - and follow my own moral compass - then the only expectations I need to live up to are my own."
– Michelle Obama

Once upon a time, there was a young boy who learned a valuable lesson from his Moral Science teacher in school. The teacher had said, "Daahine haath se kuch daan karo toh baanye haath ko pata na chale", which means, give with your right hand in such a manner that even your left hand doesn't know about it. The boy took this lesson to heart and decided to live his life by this moral code.

One day, the boy was given 100 rupees by his parents to buy some stationery from the local shop. As he was on his way to the shop, he noticed a small, underprivileged child looking at him with hungry eyes. The boy realised that this child couldn't afford food, let alone go to school. His heart went out to the hungry child.

Instead of using the money to buy stationery, the boy bought food for the child, ensuring that he wouldn't go to bed hungry that night. When he returned home without the items he was supposed to buy, his parents questioned him. When they asked for the money back, the boy hesitated.

His parents insisted on knowing how he had used the money, and with a heavy heart, the boy finally revealed the truth. He told them

about the hungry child he had met and how he couldn't bear to see someone suffer.

Initially, his parents were surprised and a bit upset about his decision. But as they listened to his heartfelt explanation, they felt proud of their compassionate and empathetic child. The boy, however, was conflicted. While he had made others happy, he felt like he had not upheld his parents' expectations.

This story highlights a common dilemma many of us face in life. We often find ourselves torn between doing something that makes us proud of our values and actions and doing something to please others or gain their approval. The boy chose to follow his values and be proud of himself, even if it meant facing disappointment from others.

> The lesson here is that it's important to make decisions that align with your values and principles, even if they don't always make everyone else happy. Being true to yourself and your moral code is a source of inner strength and pride, and it's an essential aspect of living a meaningful and authentic life.

36

ARROWS AND TRIGGERS

"The ability to Stop and think before reacting to triggers is crucial to build emotional strength."
— **Sanjay Dua**

Remember the time when Doordarshan would telecast epics like Ramayana and Mahabharata every Sunday? We would eagerly wait for the show, containing all our excitement.

There would often be a sequence depicting the battles fought between the two warring parties where a series of arrows would be shot from both sides. Whenever an arrow was launched from one side, the enemies would answer it with another one. Arrows that were strong and launched with power would hit the target, but the weak ones would not be able to keep up and would wither.

These arrows are symbolic of the triggers that come racing towards us, every day in life. We are the ones who need to face every trigger, big or small. It depends on you, whether to handle the trigger well or fall apart from its force. These superficial triggers are in the form of undesirable reactions and comments from the external world. If you are internally strong, they will do little harm to you and your well-being. However, if you are not as strong from within, even the smallest of triggers will crush you altogether.

People often answer a trigger (for example, a comment) with another trigger (another comment). This is because they always want to portray themselves as powerful, and in a bid to win.

Remember, life is to live, and not win. Real strength is not in answering a trigger with another, but in standing strong and not falling apart despite the triggers. Once you embrace this transformation, you shall be capable of handling every trigger, irrespective of how big or small it is.

37

WHERE THE
SOLUTION LIES

*"Before you look to blame another,
always look within!"*
– Leon Brown

With the onset of the winter season, a teacher once had a delicious breakfast full of green vegetables, and then set off for work. When he reached school, his students started laughing and making fun of him. Unaware of the reason, the teacher scolded the kids. He filed a complaint letter at the principal's office. The children's parents were called, saying that their kids lacked values of respect.

Dejected and depressed, the teacher returned home. When he discussed the entire incident with his family members, they too, surprisingly, started laughing. Already disappointed because of what happened in school, the teacher felt even his family was acting insensitively.

He locked himself inside the washroom. He started having negative feelings about his students, and his family too, for the way all of them behaved with him. When he washed his face and looked in the mirror, he realised that the spinach he had eaten in his morning meal was still stuck in his teeth. Because of this, his

students and his family had laughed at him.

A major realisation dawned upon him. He understood all these individuals were laughing for a reason, and that they were not the problem. Rather, the issue was with the way he looked.

Compare this with your everyday life. Whenever you face a hurdle, you would first pinpoint external sources. Instead of introspecting and looking within yourself, it is easy to blame the outer world.

> The day you start looking for the solution inside yourself, you will feel the difference. When you change, the entire world changes!

38

THE PICKLE JAR THEORY

*"Good things happen when you get your
priorities straight."*
– Scott Caan

Many of us enjoy the delicious taste of pickles. If you have ever observed the process of preparing pickles, you would know it involves many ingredients. There are mango slices, lemon slices, chilies, and lots of spices. Once all these are put together and made ready, the mixture is transferred into a container. Finally, oil is poured into it, so that the pickle is ready for consumption in a few days.

But imagine, if you pour the oil first into the container, there wouldn't be space to accommodate the other big ingredients.

Oil is a very flexible ingredient, which adjusts itself, no matter how big or small the space is.

Consider these ingredients as small parts of your life. Always focus and place those things on priority which are more important. On the other hand, oil resembles those parts that easily fit into the space in between other things. You must never leave the vital parts unattended, since they should be on your list first.

Focus on the bigger, more important aspects. The others will adjust themselves to the entire ecosystem automatically. Keep your priority tasks first, and your mundane activities will find a place. All you need to do is identify the mangoes, lemons, and chilies!

❖ ❖ ❖ ❖

39

VALUE RELATIONSHIPS LIKE MONEY

"Just as we instinctively protect our money, we must guard our relationships with care, respect, and effort."
– Sanjay Dua

Have you ever seen someone drop their money by mistake on the ground, and then quickly pick it up and put it back in their pocket? It's like a reflex action, right? Well, sometimes, we do something similar with our relationships.

Think about how often you say sorry when you make a mistake, hurting your friends or family. The more you apologise, the more you show that you care about those relationships. It's a lot like how you treat your money. You can earn money and spend it on things you like, and that's valid. But what really matters is how much you value your money and your relationships in your heart.

Our relationships need us to navigate and steer them in the way we want. Often, our words and actions show how much family and friends mean to us.

Just like you would like to keep your money safe and secure in your pocket, follow that in your relationships too. Value them and preserve the memories they have created for you.

40

HEROES

I once came across a gentleman, with whom I had a brief interaction. He said, "My life is absolutely devoid of any meaning, purpose, or value." On asking him why, he replied, "See, neither am I able to achieve something for my own self, nor am I of use to someone else or society. So, my presence or absence doesn't really matter."

This is not just the case with this gentleman. Rather, many people are often entangled in such negative thoughts about themselves. The world currently has over 8 billion people in its population. Every one of these 8 billion people has their own story.

In each of these stories, you will find the presence of a hero, be it in the form of a spouse, a friend, a parent, a teacher, or even a celebrity figure. Irrespective of how the story unfolds, a hero always finds a place in each of these people's lives.

If you think carefully, you would also have one such hero in your life, someone who has affected or transformed your life in surprising ways. Often, you don't realise how your words, actions, or even lifestyle habits profoundly impact someone else. Who knows, you might be the hero of someone's story!

Undoubtedly, one such story in the Universe exists, where you are playing the main character.

> Today, identify the hero in your life and make that phone call, or write that letter, thanking and telling them how they have shaped your life in the most unique way possible!

41

KEEP THE VESSEL CLEAN

"The world is full of goodness, but to truly experience it, we must first cleanse our own minds and hearts. A pure perspective, like a clean pan, allows us to embrace life's beauty without the stain of past negativity."
— Sanjay Dua

Once four friends decided to make some coffee together. They gathered the ingredients and began the process. As they poured the milk into the pan, they quickly realised that something was wrong. The milk had gone sour, and it didn't taste good at all.

Thinking it was an issue with the quality of the milk, they decided to go outside and buy a better one. They returned with a fresh batch of milk, poured it into the pan, and once again, it turned sour. This happened a few more times, leaving them puzzled and confused.

What they didn't realise was that the pan they were using had not been properly cleaned. There were leftover stains and soap residues in the pan, which were contaminating the fresh milk and making it sour. Once they cleaned the pan thoroughly, they could finally make their delicious cups of coffee.

Similarly, in our lives and interactions with the world, there are many beautiful things about nature and people. However, sometimes, our minds and hearts are like that unclean pan. We

carry assumptions, preconceived notions, judgments, negative memories, and other forms of negativity. These negative thoughts and feelings can sour our experiences and prevent us from enjoying the beauty of the world and the goodness in others.

To fully embrace and appreciate the good things that life and people have to offer, we need to cleanse our hearts and minds from negativity. Just like the clean pan allowed the milk to remain fresh and tasty, clearing our minds of negativity enables us to enjoy the full beauty and goodness of the universe and the people in it. It's a reminder that sometimes, it's our own perspective and mindset that can sour the wonderful things life has to offer.

42

IMPRINTING BELIEFS

– Sanjay Dua

When kids are small, they go through many phases before learning to walk well; they crawl, take baby steps, and try to balance themselves. They gradually learn to walk, but in the process, they often hurt themselves from the corners of sharp objects like tables, for example.

When kids get hurt, it is very common for a parent or guardian to behave in a certain way. Often the parent hits that table, showing the child that they hit back the table which had caused harm to the kid.

Subconsciously, the child starts believing that it is fair to hit back the table and feel good about it too.

While parents don't intentionally plant such beliefs in their children, the kids start receiving them on a subconscious level. As the child grows up and attends school, college, and beyond, such beliefs often remain with them. These beliefs teach them that, once they hurt people who harmed them in some way, they can feel better. Unfortunately, they pick up on these beliefs and follow them in situations even in adult life.

This is the major cause of sadness for so many of us. You must know what beliefs you wish to carry forward, and which ones to unlearn or relearn. Otherwise, you would start deriving pleasure by being the cause of someone's sadness. So, take some time to unlearn and relearn some subconscious beliefs that are silently limiting and pulling you back in life.

PART VI
FOCUS, GROWTH, AND PRODUCTIVITY

43

DISTRACTION

– E. Habib

There is a record of an interesting incident back in 1925; there were some professionals who had to work with a lot of focus and concentration. But they were facing a peculiar and big problem – there was a lot of noise outside that kept bothering them and ruining their work.

To help them, someone came up with a brilliant idea. They designed a special helmet that, when worn, blocked out all the noise from the outside world. The only thing it had was a little pipe to let in fresh air for breathing.

Now, when we work, we often get distracted too. To understand this, try something: write down on a piece of paper how many times you get distracted by things happening around you, like noise or people. But also, notice how many times there are no outside distractions, yet your mind still wanders from your work.

You might be surprised to find that about 70% of the time, it's your own thoughts and feelings that distract you.

It's like having a lot of noise inside your heart and mind, with different thoughts about different things pulling your attention away from your work

So, the important thing here isn't just to control the distractions from the outside world, but also to manage the distractions coming from within yourself. It's like wearing that helmet for your mind, to help you stay focused on what you're doing.

44

FOCUS

Think about the balloons we used to play with when we were kids. There were two types. The first type was the one we blew up ourselves by taking a deep breath and filling it with air from our lungs. The second type was the helium balloon, filled with a special gas that makes it float upwards because helium is lighter than regular air.

Now, imagine that we are like these balloons. The first type, the one we filled with our breath, would go up and down. People could push it down, and it might go up again. It didn't have a clear path.

But the second type, the helium balloon, is different. It knows exactly where it's going – up. It has a clear destination.

Similarly, the feelings, emotions, thoughts, and actions we have are like the air inside these balloons. It depends on us whether we want to be like the first balloon, moving in different directions and getting influenced by others, or if we want to be like the second balloon, having a clear path and direction for our life.

Both balloons will eventually run out of air, and both will have to move on in life. The difference lies in how we choose to move forward. So, the question is, will you be like the first balloon or the second one? Will you let life toss you around, or will you have a clear view of your destination and purpose?

45

CONSISTENCY

"What separates the good players from the greats people remember is consistency."
– Ryan Mason

Summers were the most anticipated time for anyone during childhood, the reason being holidays! Yes, summer vacations would be so exciting as we would stay at home and enjoy ourselves, taking a break from usual classes.

We would often feel bored during vacations, as we didn't have to study, nor did we have any other pressure of assignments and deadlines. Finally, convinced that there is nothing else to do, we would resort to cleaning our house. Fuelled with enthusiasm, we would get the house in order and make it spic and span. It felt like an achievement when the house looked neat after consistently cleaning for days.

However, the energy would die down after a few days. The same corners we cleaned some time back would again be covered with dust and dirt. But seeing it did not affect us anymore, and we turned a blind eye to the dust.

Whenever you start something new in life, say a hobby or a habit like meditation, there is so much excitement in the beginning. But as you pursue it, the enthusiasm fades away after a few days, and you don't approach it with that level of interest anymore. At that point, all you need is consistency.

Once you start practising something with consistency and discipline, no matter how motivated you are, you end up doing it every single day. Your practice becomes so strong in this process, that whenever you feel it is a dull day and you won't be able to do it, you actually end up doing it better.

> While motivation and excitement are great, the value of being consistent is the most vital aspect. If you combine all these together, you will find yourself doing so much better everywhere.

46

PATIENCE AND PERSEVERANCE

"In a world of instant gratification, patience is becoming a lost art. The joy of anticipation, the thrill of waiting, and the value of perseverance remind us that not everything meaningful comes in an instant- some things are worth the wait."
— Sanjay Dua

Back in the day, there was a TV show called 'Tahqeeqat' that used to air on Doordarshan. People who watched it would eagerly wait for the next episode, and there was a sense of excitement and anticipation. The show used to end at 9:30 PM, and if you wanted to know what happened next, you had to wait for an entire week. So, you can imagine how the viewers waited in suspense, discussing theories with friends, and counting down the days until the next episode.

Now, let's fast forward to today's world. You don't have to wait a week or even a day to watch the next episode of your favourite show. With the advent of streaming services, you can binge-watch an entire series in a single night. The convenience of instant access to content has become a norm.

However, this instant gratification has had its impact. It has changed the way we experience curiosity and eagerness. The excitement of waiting and the anticipation of what's to come have

somewhat diminished. In the world of immediate availability, our mental well-being, happiness, mindfulness, and focus have been affected.

> We've become used to getting everything we want right away, and this can make us less patient and less appreciative of the small joys of anticipation. It's essential to balance the convenience of instant access with the value of patience and the anticipation that comes with waiting for something special. This way, we can continue to enjoy the simple pleasures of life and maintain a healthy balance in our fast-paced world.

47

BREAKING LIMITS: REDEFINING WHAT YOU CAN DO

"Don't limit yourself. Many people limit themselves to what they think they can do.
You can go as far as your mind lets you.
What you believe, remember, you can achieve."
– Mary Kay Ash

I once accompanied my parents to the railway station to see them off. In their luggage, there was a huge piece, weighing about 25 kilograms. Being someone who never lifts weights, I was worried that I wouldn't be able to lift the luggage and place it onto the luggage rack. However, when the time came to do so, I tried, and I did it.

Another instance had me dropping my child at the bus stop, just as his school bus was about to come, my son realised he had forgotten something important at home. So, I had to run back, fetch it, and hand it over to him at the bus stop. This made me realise that I could run fast covering quite a distance in very little time.

Before these two incidents, I had believed I could just jog or cycle. But when these situations compelled me to step out of my comfort zone and do something different, I understood I could run and lift too.

It is all about the perceptions you feed into your mind, which make you believe that you can or cannot do something. Just with a little effort, you can actually change those limiting beliefs. You might have heard many people saying that they can't change. But these are just wrong thoughts that pull them away from discovering their true potential.

Just as a sculptor starts with a rough block of stone, not truly knowing the possibilities but believing in them, and with each precise strike of the chisel, the masterpiece within begins to emerge. But if the chisel becomes dull and the sculptor doesn't sharpen it, the details remain hidden, and progress slows.

Just like the sculptor must continuously refine their tool, we must refine our beliefs-challenging our limits, unlearning doubts, and carving out our full potential. In the same way, if you keep unlearning wrong beliefs and relearn new perspectives, you can achieve all that you can imagine, and beyond.

48

SEVEN STONES

"Step with care and great tact. And remember
life's a great balancing act."

– Dr. Seuss

Back in childhood, we would spend time with friends playing Pitthoo, or Seven Stones, a nostalgic game. You had to knock over a stack of stones with a ball, and then rebuild the entire stack once again before the opponents hit you with the ball. The team that would do this first, would eventually become the winner.

However, winning this game demanded many different skills. You needed to be prompt and active, have a good aim, and collaborate well with your team members. You even had to be alert and cautious about the ball not hitting you from the back! If you skilfully ticked all these checklists and rebuilt the stack with perfect balance, you would win.

In life, we are often faced with situations where we have to take care of many different things all at once, just like in the game of Pitthoo. Sometimes, the situation is against you, or sometimes, your physical condition doesn't allow you to be your best. Sometimes even the situation doesn't unfold in the way you thought it would.

With all these hurdles, if you successfully take control of every tough situation, you can win the 'Pitthoo' of life. If you can balance your life like those seven stones, you become the winner, just like in the game. It is easy to cross the ocean when the waters are calm. The real test lies in being calm and performing your best even when the currents are violent.

49

MASTER OF DESTINY

Once upon a time, in a bustling city, there lived a young woman. She was an ordinary girl, or so she thought until she came across a secret that changed her life forever. This secret was not buried in the pages of dusty old books or hidden in the far corners of the earth. Instead, it was a revelation that dawned upon her.

She had always been a curious soul, constantly seeking new experiences and adventures. She believed that life was meant to be lived to the fullest. However, despite her enthusiasm, she often found herself tangled in a web of self-doubt, anxiety, and negative thoughts that seemed to control her.

One day she was reading a book where it was written:

"You control your own mind, and it's not the other way around. By recognising this, you can learn to manage your mind through practice and by developing various skills, similar to how you improve your physical abilities."

As the days turned into weeks and weeks into months, the woman embarked on a journey of self-discovery. She practiced mindfulness, meditation, and various mental exercises. Slowly, she learned to recognise the negative thought patterns that had

held her back for so long. It was as if she had uncovered a hidden treasure within herself.

With each passing day, her confidence grew. She was no longer a prisoner of her own thoughts but the master of her own destiny. She realised that she could steer her mind in any direction she desired. Her friends and family saw the radiance in her eyes and the calmness in her behaviour. They were inspired by her journey and they too joined her in the quest to master their wandering minds.

A city that was once only filled with stressed souls began to transform into a hub of mental well-being. People realised that they held the power to control their minds. They understood that by nurturing their thoughts and emotions, they could become the architects of their happiness.

> This woman's story reminds us that we are not victims of our thoughts but creators of our reality. With dedication and practice, anyone can harness the incredible power within their minds and walk towards a brighter future.

50

THE POWER OF BELIEF

*"Never give up, for that is just the place and
time that the tide will turn."*
– Harriet Beecher Stowe

An article talked about an experiment that was undertaken about fifty years ago. A few rats were taken and put into a test tube filled with water. The aim of the experiment was to test how long the rats would be able to stay in the water. The rats constantly tried to come out of the water, but they were not able to. **After fifteen minutes, it was found that the rats were almost about to die,** which is when they were taken out of the test tube. Ultimately, they got saved.

They were once again put into the tube, to see how long they could survive before they had to be taken out of the water. Surprisingly, **the rats were able to keep themselves in the water this time for almost sixty hours!** The energy their body had, to be able to survive, had increased manifold.

Someone saved the rats from death the first time. When they were put back into the tube, they knew that if they kept fighting for survival, someone would definitely come and save them. This is where the power of belief comes into play. This belief helped the rats to increase their body resistance from fifteen minutes to sixty hours.

The same applies to human beings. You must never sit idle;
you must fight your problems. You need to put in the extra
effort, but with the hope that someday, the things
that are meant for you will come to you. There would be
some Universal energy to help you, but for that,
you must keep fighting.

51

SELF-WORTH

"Like Gold your Worth is non-negotiable, You are Worthy always, no matter what your physical or material circumstances."
– Sanjay Dua

When a stone is in a broken state, you wouldn't see it as something with a lot of value. But when it is shaped into a definite form, its worth is very visible. On being shaped, its worth and value increase heavily, contrary to that of its broken condition.

On the contrary, gold, in every form whatsoever, is considered to be valuable and worthy. No matter if it is broken into pieces or shaped into an absolute form, it doesn't lose its value at all. We see that gold doesn't fall in value on being broken apart, unlike a stone. It is considered a highly valuable metal, irrespective of its condition.

> Just like we recognise the value of metals like gold, similarly, we must be able to define and measure our own value and self-worth. This term doesn't only refer to the amount of wealth one possesses, and the net worth they have in terms of money, but the values they have grown up to imbibe. One's beliefs, lifestyle practices, and value system are the real tools to measure true value and impact.

PART VII

SOCIAL BEHAVIOUR AND COMMUNICATION

52

POSITIVE COMMUNICATION

"Words shape thoughts, and thoughts shape actions. When we shift from fear-driven warnings to positive encouragement, we don't just communicate- we inspire, empower, and build confidence."
– Sanjay Dua

Imagine a young person who's always been told, "Don't eat that, or you'll fall sick. Don't get wet in the rain, or you'll catch a fever. Please drive safely, and don't try to do anything else, or you'll end up on the street." These are the kinds of warnings they've grown up hearing from concerned family and friends.

As humans, we tend to use this kind of negative narrative when we want to convince someone to be careful. It's not our fault; it's just how our brains have developed over thousands of years. Back in the early days of human civilisation, people had to be cautious to survive. They lived alongside wild animals and faced various dangers, so our brains evolved to be cautious and alert to potential threats.

But here's the important part: if we put in a little effort, we can learn to explain things in a positive way.

Whether we want to work effectively in a team or convince someone of something, we don't always have to resort to negative

language. There are many ways to have a conversation that focuses on the positive side of things and encourages people to cooperate and excel.

> So, while it's natural for us to have a built-in tendency to be cautious, we can also harness the power of positive communication to inspire and motivate ourselves and those around us. It's all about finding the right balance between being safe and embracing a positive outlook.

53

CHOICE OF WORDS

"Handle them carefully, for words have more
power than atom bombs."
– Pearl Strachan Hurd

Imagine it's a new day, and you decide to do a simple experiment. You take a cold lemon from the fridge and feel its coolness in your hand. When you smell it, you notice a fresh and strong scent. Curiously, you slice the lemon in half and smell it again, and this time, the fragrance is even stronger.

Then, you decide to squeeze one of the lemon halves, and a drop of its sour juice touches your tongue, making your senses come alive. But here's the interesting part: even if you didn't have the lemon in your hand or the juice on your tongue, just by hearing about it, your brain would still be tricked into imagining the taste of the lemon as if it were real. It's like your mind can create the flavour even without the actual lemon.

This happens because your brain is pretty amazing. Words, when put together in a story, can make your body react as if something real is happening. It's not about having the lemon; it's about the words that describe it. This shows how powerful language can be.

Words can't change the real world, but they can change how you see and understand it. The way you talk and the words you use affect how you think.

It's like words conduct a symphony in your brain, and this dance between language and thinking shows how incredible your mind is.

I have been reading a book called 'The Silva Mind Control' by Jose Silva. This book explores how stories can shape your thoughts and beliefs.

> The words you read are like food for your mind; they can reshape how you think and even change your view of the world. It's like words can paint a new picture in your mind and create a different reality.
> Choose your words wisely, for they have the power one can't even imagine!

54

AN EMPOWERING NARRATIVE

"Words shape worlds - choose them
to uplift, not to break."
– Sanjay Dua

A long time ago, when I was in the 7th grade, I had a Sanskrit teacher who cared a lot about his students. One day, he noticed that I wasn't focusing on my studies as I should have been. I used to sit at the back of the class and wasn't putting in the effort I was capable of.

One day, my teacher called me aside and said, "Sanjay, nowadays, you're not concentrating on your studies. You're sitting at the back, and it's like "genhu ke saath ghun bhi pis jaata hai'." (an ancient Hindi proverb full of wisdom meaning that even the good people get affected by keeping the wrong company) He told me that he expected better from me.

The way my teacher addressed me and the words he used left a deep impact on me. He was honest and straightforward, but he didn't use harsh or negative language. Instead, he empowered me with the truth.

104

What this story teaches us is the importance of the narrative we use when we want to inspire change in someone. The way we describe and communicate things can either make or break a person's spirit. When you're encouraging someone to change or improve themselves, using a positive and empowering narrative can make all the difference. It helps the person believe that they have the potential to do better, and it can be a powerful motivator for positive change.

55

AUTHENTICITY OVER APPEARANCE

"You can NEVER be like someone else!
Just be yourself and you will find that you'll be much
happier that way and accomplish more as well."
– Anonymous

Once upon a time, in a quiet little pond, a duck gave birth to a group of adorable ducklings. Among them was one duckling that looked a little different from the rest. Her feathers were not as sleek, and her size was a bit bigger compared to her siblings. When she tried to swim and play with the other ducklings, they would often tease her, calling her the 'ugly duckling'.

One day, feeling hurt and discouraged, the so-called 'ugly duckling' decided to leave her home in search of a place where she could belong. She wandered through the countryside until she found a beautiful pond where elegant swans were gracefully swimming.

She watched the swans from afar, longing to join them. But she hesitated, convinced that she was not good-looking like the other swans. The memory of being called the 'ugly duckling' haunted her.

One friendly swan noticed the lonely duckling and approached her. The swan told her that she was very good-looking and invited

her to play with the swan group. The duckling, feeling unsure and self-conscious, refused, thinking the swans were just making fun of her.

Undeterred, the kind swan gave her a piece of advice. "Look at your reflection in the water," the swan said, "You might be surprised."

Taking the swan's suggestion, the duckling gazed at her reflection in the pond. To her astonishment, she saw that she had transformed into a beautiful swan herself. She had been a swan all along but hadn't realised it. She had judged herself based on her past experiences and the unkind words of others.

This story conveys an essential message: Just like the 'ugly duckling', many of us may not realise our uniqueness and potential. People often judge others based on appearances, but the true value lies in the qualities within us.

> Self-discovery and self-acceptance are powerful tools for understanding our worth and embracing our unique qualities. It reminds us that we should not let external judgments define our self-worth but instead appreciate the inner qualities that make us special.

56

RESPECT OR FEAR?

*"Fear forces obedience, but respect nurtures commitment.
When we move from doing things out of fear to
embracing them with understanding, we
transform obligation into genuine dedication."*
– Sanjay Dua

Imagine you are a young child, and one evening, you need to go into a dark room to fetch something. Your older sibling, in an attempt to keep you from going there, playfully warns you, "Don't go in there; there might be a ghost!" You get a bit scared and decide not to enter the dark room.

As you grow up, you often hear similar warnings and instructions. You're told, "Study properly, or you'll fail," and "Don't disturb your parents while they're working, or they'll stop your pocket money." These messages begin to shape your behaviour. You avoid dark rooms because you're afraid of ghosts. You study not because you're eager to learn, but because you're afraid of failing. You respect your parents, not out of genuine appreciation, but out of fear that they might take away your pocket money.

These early narratives, instilled through fear, become deeply ingrained in your mind. Fear influences your actions, and you continue to do things because you're afraid of the consequences.

But as you grow even older, you begin to understand the difference between fear and respect. You realise that fear might push you

to do things, but it often leads to stress, anxiety, and a sense of obligation. On the other hand, respect and genuine dedication come from within. When you respect your studies, your parents, or any task you undertake, you approach them with a willingness to learn and grow. Your efforts become more meaningful, and your commitment to them strengthens over time.

The story underscores the importance of recognising the difference between actions driven by fear and those motivated by genuine respect and dedication. It reminds us that when we act out of respect and a true desire to learn or grow, our efforts and achievements tend to be more enduring and fulfilling.

57

FLEETING MOMENTS: LASTING CONSEQUENCES

"Life isn't just shaped by the time we invest,
but by the moments we choose to show up.
The smallest lapse in presence can overshadow years
of effort-because some moments, once missed,
can never be reclaimed."
– Sanjay Dua

We've all experienced this phenomenon at home-one that is so common yet carries a deep lesson about life. Remember when our mothers would put a pot of milk on the stove and ask us to keep an eye on it so that it wouldn't boil over? We would stand there, eyes fixed on the pot, waiting for that final moment when the milk would rise. But no matter how intently we watched, it seemed to take forever. Eventually, our patience would wear thin, and we'd get distracted-maybe stepping away for just a moment to do something else. And right at that very instant, we'd hear a loud call from the kitchen-"The milk has spilled!"-followed by the inevitable scolding for not being attentive enough to such a simple task.

This small yet familiar incident mirrors a crucial reality of life. Whether in our personal relationships, at work, or in business, responsibilities demand continuous awareness and focus. You might be present for people most of the time, offering support and standing by them through their journey. But when a crucial moment arrives-one where your presence truly matters-and you're not there, all your past efforts can be overshadowed.

In friendships, you may be the one who always checks in, listens, and shares laughter. But if you're absent when your friend needs you the most, it could leave a lasting gap in the relationship. In leadership, you could be making great contributions, but missing a critical decision or failing to step up at the right moment could cost you the trust and confidence of your team.

Life doesn't just test us through long-term commitments; it also tests us in fleeting moments that define trust, reliability, and significance. Just like the milk on the stove, you never know exactly when that boiling point will arrive, but if you stay mindful and committed, you won't miss the moment when it truly counts.

58

A MINDFUL CONVERSATION

"When we get too caught up in the busyness of the world, we lose connection with one another – and ourselves."
– Jack Kornfield

Some time ago, my son had his exams just around the corner. He told me that he wanted to ask me something, as his tests were about to begin. I was scrolling through my phone, but I told him to go on and ask me the question. But he still said, "Papa, meri baat suno."

When I told him that I was listening, he still insisted that I keep aside my phone, look him in the eyes, and listen to him. I complied and spoke to him for about ten minutes. Once I did this, I realised I was actually having a proper conversation with him after ages. It took so long for those ten minutes to end!

The moment I kept my phone away; I spoke to him with my complete mind and attention. He too was able to dedicate his entire energy to the conversation, ultimately leading to quality time spent.

Whenever someone asks you for your time, they are not merely asking for your 'time', but also your 'energy' and 'attention'.

There is a difference. If you spend two hours with someone, but keep checking your emails, or make phone calls in between, you

are not really present in that conversation. The other person might even feel that you were not there for them during those hours.

> On the other hand, even a few minutes spent with someone without the constant buzzing of mobile notifications will satisfy him/her. This is because you had a mindful conversation, where you centred all your energy.
> Time is not as important as the energy you fuel it with.

59

STRENGTH

*"Greatness is not built by fixing weaknesses,
but by mastering strengths."*
– Sanjay Dua

Let me take you to a cricket academy brimming with many aspiring cricketers, who practised day in and day out. Amongst the many kids, I especially want to tell you about about one particular kid. The coach worked hard on this kid's bowling skills for many days, however, the kid only took an interest in batting.

After a few months, the kid altogether left bowling. Even the coach agreed that he was a very good batsman. What really panned out was that the coach had understood the kid's real strength. He had realised that his potential lay in batting, rather than bowling. Therefore, he decided to work hard to enhance and improve his area of strength.

In various phases of our lives, be it school, college, or corporate houses, all the conversation revolves around where people lack. It is pivoted around their weaknesses. What is often ignored is the strengths that people possess. Rarely do we see people discussing how they can capitalise on someone's strength.

> Instead of pointing at the loopholes, if we start focussing on people's strengths and improving their self-belief, life will be so much more wholesome.

Part VIII

Introspections and Reflections

60

SHAPING THE MINDSET

*"Strength isn't just about enduring challenges-it's about
facing them with purpose, dignity, and an unshakable
spirit. Life isn't just about earning a livelihood;
it's about earning respect, breaking barriers,
and paving the way for others to rise."*
– Sanjay Dua

Back in 1987, in our entire colony, my mother was the only working woman. At a time when societal norms were rigid, and women stepping out to earn a livelihood was uncommon-if not frowned upon-she had no choice but to rise to the occasion. Circumstances demanded it, and she embraced the responsibility with unwavering determination.

For 33 years, she worked relentlessly, not as someone merely fulfilling a duty, but as someone who truly owned her work. Never once did I see her lacking enthusiasm or treating her job as just a means to an end. She carried herself with a sense of purpose, a quiet resilience that spoke volumes about her character.

Her journey was far from easy, yet she never let challenges define her. Instead, she defined how to face them-with grit, grace, and an unyielding commitment to her family and work.

116

Her story teaches so many vital values that one can pursue in life:

➢ **Resilience in Adversity:** When faced with difficult circumstances, we can either surrender or rise. My mother chose to rise.

➢ **Purposeful Work Ethic:** No matter the job, what sets you apart is your attitude. She never treated her work as a burden but as a commitment, she took pride in.

➢ **Breaking Barriers:** She unknowingly became a pioneer, proving that a woman can manage both professional and personal responsibilities despite societal constraints.

➢ **Leading by Example:** Through her perseverance, she taught us that strength is not about having an easy life but about showing up every day, regardless of how hard it gets.

> Her journey wasn't just about earning a livelihood-it was about shaping a mindset, setting an example, and proving that when life pushes you, you push back harder.

THE VICIOUS CYCLE
OF ZERO

"Life isn't about how many zeroes you add, but what stands before them. Impact, purpose, and meaning outlast every number."
— **Sanjay Dua**

Each time a batsman walks onto the field, adjusting his gloves, scanning the field placements, and feeling the weight of expectations, it's like being a newcomer. No matter how many centuries he has scored, how many matches he has won, the moment he stands at zero, there's an uneasiness.

The scoreboard shows nothing against his name, no past glory matters, the slate is wiped clean and the only thing on his mind is getting off the mark. That first run is a relief. A simple single, yet it feels like the most important run of the innings.

Zero has that strange effect on people. No one wants it-neither in cricket nor in life. No one wants zero money, zero progress, zero recognition. The fear of being at zero makes people restless, pushing them to move forward.

But here's where the irony begins-once a number gets attached to zero, everything changes.

A salary of 10 feels small, but add a zero, and it becomes 100. Businesses start with 1 lakh worth of money but dream of adding

more zeros to reach 10 lakhs, then 1 crore. The pursuit of zeroes becomes endless. More zeroes mean more success, more status, and more validation. People convince themselves that the next zero will bring ultimate happiness.

But what they don't realise is that life itself is a cycle of zero. It begins at zero and, no matter how many zeroes are added along the way, ultimately returns to zero.

A billionaire and a beggar both leave the world with nothing.

The only thing that remains is not the number of zeroes, but the one before them-the impact created, the moments lived, and the meaning found in the journey.

Just like in cricket, in life too, getting off zero is important,
but beyond that, it's not just about adding zeroes-
it's about playing the innings wisely.

62

THE BALANCE SHEET

Fifteen years ago, when I received my first salary, a beautiful and satisfying message appeared on my phone. It said, "Your account has been credited…". This acted as a booster message, a notification that reminded me of the hard work I was doing, and the fact that I was receiving something in return.

Ask yourself, do you write such motivational notifications to improve yourself?

Each of us is faced with so many issues, some struggle with maintaining their mental peace, some have social media addiction, and so on. But what if we start pushing ourselves towards improvement through such messages?

Today, take a notepad and write down your achievement in the form of a short, inspiring message. For example, if you successfully meditate for 15 minutes, write that "15 minutes of meditation have been credited to your life". Similarly, if you are able to control an urge for addiction of some kind (like gambling) for three whole days, write it down on your notepad.

What happens in this simple process is that you indirectly send messages and motivations to your mind that you are on the right path to achieving your goals. On the way, you are also getting these little notifications that push you to explore your potential. Give yourself the motivation that reinforces the fact that you are improving day in and day out. Try making the balance sheet of life today!

63

CRACKS

Two kids were painting vases in their art class.

One was excited to make their vase look perfect, imagining neat patterns and vibrant colours. The other was equally eager, but as they worked, their vase accidentally slipped and broke into pieces. Devastated, they sat quietly, ready to give up.

Seeing their disappointment, the teacher walked over and said, "Don't give up just yet. What if you used these cracks to make something unique? Highlight them, turn them into part of the design, and see what happens."

With some hesitation but a spark of hope, the child began gluing the pieces back together. They painted the cracks with golden strokes, letting the flaws become part of the story. By the end, the vase wasn't just repaired-it was transformed into something truly beautiful and unique.

When it came time to showcase the vases, the unbroken vase looked flawless. But it was the once-broken vase, with its golden cracks, that everyone admired the most.

Life isn't about having everything perfect. We all face
cracks-mistakes, failures, or setbacks. But it's how we respond
that matters. When we embrace the cracks
and turn them into something meaningful, we create
beauty out of imperfection.
Remember, the cracks in your journey might just be the
most powerful part of your story.

A POSITIVE LENS

"Remember that everything that is happening around you, good or bad, is in some way conspiring to help you."
— Debasish Mridha

When kids are young and curious about things in their vicinity unaware of the consequences, they tend to touch and play with fire. They are intrigued to touch it. When they try this, their parents often stop them and pull them away from it. However, they still go back to try touching the fire, and they do this a number of times, every time being stopped from doing so. They feel a sense of frustration every time their parents scold them for such naughtiness.

Just like these kids, we often feel depressed and frustrated when we are unable to achieve a goal. It could be clearing an exam, reaching a sales figure in the business, and so on. On failure, you start attracting negative emotions, feeling you are not good enough.

Remember, there is always a reason something happens. The kids, while growing up, learn why their parents kept stopping them from touching fire. Similarly, you will also understand why something happened in its own way much later.

Always believe that the Universe is doing its best to signal what works for you and what doesn't. Think through the positive lens, and keep faith that if something doesn't work, something else happens. If you put in all your efforts and tried every way to achieve something, but still in vain, know that there is a reason for it.

65

THE AUTOPILOT MIRAGE

"Life begins where autopilot ends. Step out of routine, embrace new experiences, and make every moment truly count."
– Sanjay Dua

Life is all about making choices at every stage, every situation. You will find you are faced with the instance of making choices every now and then. Think of this; if you are planning to travel by road, you will consult with friends about the terrain, the duration of the journey, and more. You want to make a decision and choice that gives you the comfort of smooth and easy travel.

The world is often addicted to the autopilot mode of functioning in daily life. People are comfortable in their routine lives, with nothing new to experiment or toy with. The mere thought of a new experience challenges and scares them. But the real excitement of enjoying life lies in those very experiences.

> Remember, you have one life. Don't get caught up in the autopilot mirage. Embark on new experiences, and make every moment count!

66

THE LIFE CYCLE

"Just like a white shirt gathers dust through the day, life collects experiences-some bright, some dark. Regular healing, like daily washing, keeps the soul fresh, ready to embrace each new day with clarity and peace."
— *Sanjay Dua*

Imagine you wear a white shirt and leave for work in the morning. All through the day, you travel to places, attend meetings, and do so many tasks. When you return back home in the evening, you will see that the shirt isn't white anymore. Rather, it has turned another shade, owing to the dust that has settled onto it during the day. You then send the shirt for laundry, so that it can be cleaned and made tidy again for the next day.

Now, you apply this same concept to your life. When you are born into this world, you are just like a neat white shirt, without any stains or marks, ready to experience life. As you grow up through the life cycle, people comment on you, you react to them, and so on. Such instances paint that shirt in various colours, through every situation.

Just like that white shirt needs washing, your life too needs healing every day. If something bad happens today, and you don't sort it, healing it after five years will be tough. But if you regularly heal yourself with spirituality, gratitude, exercises, and other such lifestyle habits, you will attract so much more peace and positivity.

67

THE TRAP

Examinations were around the corner and soon approaching for a batch of children. One student sincerely prepared and worked hard for the upcoming tests. He religiously learned and revised repeatedly. However, he, by mistake, missed studying one chapter from the syllabus.

On the other hand, another student's preparation was not very elaborate. He only went through and practised some basic chapters from here and there.

Destiny was such that the question paper had most of the questions that the second student had practised randomly. It also included questions from that particular chapter which the former skipped studying.

Naturally, the first student scored less and the latter scored very well, even though he didn't prepare sincerely. The child who scored less felt sad, as so much preparation went in vain. His teacher, however, told him that his concept was very strong and it would help him later in life.

Fate followed the teacher's words and unfolded such that the student saw success in his career, as his concepts were very strong.

He didn't fall into the trap of scoring numbers in one examination, but went ahead to make it big in the test of life and career.

We often slip into chasing short-term benefits in our personal, professional, and social lives. Instead of building a meaningful relationship, for example, we choose a short-term relationship..

> Take the path that helps you derive long-term benefits and success just like that child, rather than opting for temporary, short-lived happiness.

PART IX

SOCIAL ENVIRONMENTS

68

A CAREFREE KID

*"Surround yourself with only people
who are going to lift you higher."*
– Oprah Winfrey

Six years ago, we were on a plane, and suddenly, it started shaking because of turbulence.

Everyone on the plane was petrified, except for my 6-year-old son. He was smiling and having a good time as if he thought he was swimming in the air. He didn't understand what was happening, so he stayed happy in his own world.

But as the turbulence continued, fellow passengers on the plane started crying and shouting, I noticed my son's expression changed. He went from being carefree to worried and even more anxious about the proceedings.

This story shows that in life, we often carry a happy attitude, just like the little boy. We go on with a positive outlook. But sometimes, negative influences and doubts creep in. We start questioning our decisions and the way we lead our lives. Our confidence gets shaky, and we doubt ourselves.

> So, if you want to get rid of your doubts and boost your confidence, surround yourself with people who support and strengthen you. They can help you stay positive and focused on your own path.

69

THE HONEYBEES

– Sanjay Dua

Imagine you're in a beautiful garden where there are many colourful flowers. In this garden, honeybees are buzzing around, going from one flower to another. These honeybees have a special job – to collect the sweet nectar from the flowers.

Their mission is clear. They collect nectar from various flowers, and they work really hard to gather as much as they can. Once they have collected this nectar, they bring it to their beehive. Inside the hive, they use the nectar to create honeycombs. These honeycombs are like storage units for honey.

Now, humans love honey, and it's something we keep in bottles in our homes. But here's the interesting part; the honeybees don't do all this hard work because they want money or some reward. They do it because they know it's their role, and they create something valuable that we can enjoy.

In a similar way, when we interact with people, we need to remember that everyone has their strengths (merits) and their weaknesses (demerits). Nobody is perfect; we all have our good and not-so-good sides, just like the different flowers in the garden.

If we choose to focus on the good qualities and positive aspects of the people we meet, it's a bit like the honeybees gathering the sweet nectar. We can collect the good things from each person we encounter, and over time, we can build something wonderful, just like the honeycombs.

So, let's make a promise, like an oath, to try to see the best in people and gather their positive qualities. If we do this, imagine how amazing our own 'comb' of goodness and positivity will become. It's a way to create something beautiful and valuable from the interactions and relationships in our lives.

70

THE LISTENER

"Listening is not the same as agreeing. True connection comes when we hear to understand, not just to reply or expect obedience."
– Sanjay Dua

Back in the early days when we were young, our parents would say, **"Yeh meri baat nahi sunta."** As we started attending school, our teachers would say, "Yeh meri baat nahi sunta." Growing up, we would set our minds on pursuing a career in a specific field. Even then, parents would sometimes complain of the same. Moreover, even in the professional world, our boss would make the same statement.

You would notice that in your entire life span, these words would be repeated in ninety percent of the situations you experience. But in reality, these words are very loosely used. We always assume that 'baatein sunna' (to listen to advice) is synonymous with 'baatein maanna' (to follow that advice). There is a thin line of difference between the two ideas.

If someone shares their thoughts with you, as a listener, you should listen, empathise, and try to understand the person's perspective. It is not necessary that you accept what they are talking about. Even when we share our opinions and ideas with others, we want them to not just listen, but accept and also follow what we tell them.

The day you truly understand this difference, you will improve as a listener. People will find it easier to approach you and open up about their inner feelings. This is because they would have faith in the fact that you will be there for them as a listener, acknowledging them and holding space for them without trying to critique or advise them.

> You cannot control the uncontrollable. So, the next time you share something with an individual, accept that they are just lending ears to listen to you, rather than presuming that they will follow your advice. This will solve most of your problems.

71

FRAGRANCE

– Sanjay Dua

Once upon a time, two friends were keen to plant roses in their houses and they did. One could successfully grow the plant in his house, but one couldn't. There were no signs of the plant growing at his place. Naturally, he started feeling disheartened and sad on seeing this.

After a few days, the first friend asked him, "Are you sad because your rose plant didn't grow?" the other replied, "No, I am not sad anymore. In fact, I feel amazing because the fragrance of your rose plant is reaching my house too! So, I am grateful and satisfied."

The friend whose plant had grown was surprised to hear what his friend had told him. Instead of joy, he felt resentment, now, he broke apart one of the branches of his rose plant, in an attempt to ensure that its fragrance didn't reach his friend's place. However, after three days, his plant died.

He actually tried to limit and capture the flower's fragrance, which is naturally impossible. He felt only he had the right to enjoy its fragrance and no one else and he ended up losing it all together.

Similarly, we often try to limit our goodness, skills, and values to our own selves. But doing this prevents them from doing good to ourselves and our surroundings too. Let your goodness be limitless, and inject fragrance everywhere you go!

72

INADEQUACY

– Albert Ellis

Judgment from society might be a storm you can weather, but when you become your own harshest critic, it's a different battle altogether. I found myself in the same boat, scared of facing relatives, drowning in self-doubt, and shyness that held me back from making eye contact.

The turning point? Acceptance.

Embracing my true self, vulnerabilities, and all, signalled to my mind that I was good enough, even if I wasn't entirely convinced at first. It's a journey of self-love and acknowledging that it's okay not to be perfect. In fact, imperfection is beautiful too.

My school days were marked by silence, but once I conquered the fear of failure, accepting my real self was a principle that came naturally to me. The beauty lies in realising that embracing imperfections is a catalyst for self-improvement. The journey not only toughens you up but also makes you a better version of yourself.

Once you've faced and conquered self-doubt, external opinions, be it praise or criticism, lose their power to crush you. Life becomes a more balanced journey, and you find strength in navigating its twists and turns. So, embrace yourself, flaws and all, for it might just be the key to unlocking your best self.

73

HIDDEN GEMS

— Sanjay Dua

The classroom in our childhood would consist of two different kinds of children. Some kids would raise their hands and answer every question, often being termed as the 'bright students' of the class. The teacher would also focus on them since they would be full of enthusiasm. But there would be some kids who would be silent throughout. They had potential, but they were unable to express themselves properly in class.

This culture existed in college life too, and even continued until the professional world. You might have noticed that even managers usually take suggestions and discuss strategies with employees who are proactive and take initiative. Eighty percent of individuals in all these stages, either don't feel confident enough to speak, or hesitate because of fear of judgment.

> As a leader, manager, or educator, your foremost responsibility remains to plant a seed of inspiration in those eighty percent of people. You must motivate them to contribute to conversations because you never know, who turns out to be as brainy as Einstein. Their hidden potential might just take your organisation to the heights of success.

74

INCLUSIVITY

– Sanjay Dua

On a mundane Monday morning, burdened with school expectations and a hefty bag, my friends and I embarked on the bus. Our routine Antakshari game, a melodic escape, took an unexpected turn when we invited a shy, silent junior to join, solely to balance the teams.

Initially, our motives were light-hearted, but as the game unfolded, so did the transformation of our silent teammate. When the game reached a critical point, he surprised us all by stepping up, showcasing talents we never knew he possessed. The once-shy companion emerged as a powerhouse, shifting our perception of him entirely.

As the days passed, we delved into conversations, discovering a wealth of creativity and perspective within him. The journey wasn't just about a musical game; it became a journey of cognitive restructuring. Our preconceived notions crumbled, making room for the realisation that every individual carries a unique strength and contribution.

The experience became a metaphor for the need for cognitive restructuring in the world today. To build an inclusive society, we must recognise and embrace the diverse strengths, creativity, and uniqueness each person brings to the table. It's a reminder that true richness lies in celebrating the individuality within us all.

75

COMPARISON

"Comparison blinds us to true worth. It's not who is better, but what we do that defines us-because in the end, humanity matters more than any label or title."

– Sanjay Dua

In every family that houses two or more siblings, you will find them asking their parents about who the better sibling is. They would ask, "Mai achha hu ya woh?"

We might be in school, then enter college life, and even graduate to taste the corporate world, but this term called comparison doesn't seem to leave our company. This concept has prevailed for a long period and has revolved around us for as long as one can remember.

Around 500 years ago, some priests and saints asked Guru Nanakji, "You keep preaching how one should lead life. But in your opinion, which religion is the greatest of all? Is it Hinduism, Christianity, or some other?" Hearing this intriguing question, Guru Nanakji replied, "Whether you follow Hinduism, Christianity, or hail from the Islamic community, it doesn't matter. What matters are your deeds and actions, that define you."

Guru Nanakji revealed the universal truth that religion doesn't give birth to humanity. Instead, humanity gives rise to the formation of various religions.

> Let's pray for humanity, and live for humanity, for it defines the very existence of mankind today.

76

UBUNTU

This principle finds its roots within African tribes. An instance from this context involves an anthropologist who ventured into an African tribe. In his experiment, he placed a basket of fruits beneath a tree and assembled a group of children in a line, positioned 100 meters away. Their task was to dash towards the tree, with the promise that the swiftest among them would claim the entire basket of fruits.

However, what unfolded surprised the observer profoundly. Instead of racing individually, the children joined hands and started running together. Upon reaching the tree, they shared the fruits amongst themselves. It came to light that these children had imbibed a profound teaching:

"I am because we are."

Their understanding was centred on the notion that their individual successes were connected with the well-being of their community.

This principle resonates universally. If we were to incorporate this philosophy into our lives, it could catalyse positive change within our societies. The concept underscores the importance of collective effort.
It encourages us not only to partake in competition but also to engage in collaboration. By embracing this principle, we pursue the idea of togetherness, fostering an environment where shared success is the ultimate achievement.

❖ ❖ ❖ ❖

Part X

Emotions and Energies

77

TEARS

"There is a sacredness in tears. They are not the mark of weakness but of power. They speak more eloquently than ten thousand tongues."
— **Washington Irving**

Imagine you're watching a movie, and there's a scene that's really touching or sad. As you're watching, you start to feel tears welling up in your eyes. You're not alone; many people have experienced this, including me.

Now, you might have heard that crying is a sign of being weak. People sometimes say that it's not okay to cry. But I want to tell you something important: tears are not a sign of weakness; they're a sign of your inner strength.

Think of it this way: in the world, there are only two places where you can find salt for free. One is in the vast sea, and the other is in the tears that come from people's eyes.

When you shed tears, it's not a sign that you're weak; it's a sign that you're someone who thinks and feels deeply. It shows that you have a big heart, full of emotions and empathy. Crying is your way of expressing the emotions inside you.

So, instead of feeling like crying is a weakness, embrace it as a part of your strength. Your tears are like a superpower that lets you release your feelings and connect with your emotions. Don't hold back; cry whenever you want, because it's a natural and healthy way to express your inner strength and sensitivity.

78

THE STORY OF SALT

*"Like salt in a dish, the right balance of kindness,
empathy, and humility may go unnoticed-
but without them, life loses its true flavor."*
– Sanjay Dua

Once upon a time, the scent of delicious food filled a house where spices were being mixed, and mouthwatering dishes were being prepared. After hours of preparation, the food was tasted. However, someone complained that it lacked salt.

On hearing this, the people who had prepared the food started thinking about how they had spent so many hours cooking but it ultimately didn't taste well because of a pinch of salt. In another instance, when there was excessive salt in the dishes, someone again complained that the food tasted bitter because the salt was too much in quantity.

Thus, no matter how grand your preparation is, or how much time you spend cooking, an incorrect quantity of salt always attracts criticism. Consider it a strength or weakness of salt; if it is less in quantity it is complained about, and if it is excessive in quantity, it is complained about too. However, if it is used in appropriate quantities, it blends beautifully into the food. Then, people praise the flavour of the spices, thereby neglecting the pinch of salt.

Consider salt as the soft skills that you possess in life.

Your kindness, empathy, compassion, and other values help you find balance in life. Your personality is absolutely complete when you input the correct extent of soft skills and values into it.

> Remember, life isn't just about showing your tangible, material achievements and strengths, you should also have a foundation of soft skills. This will truly help you discover a better version of yourself.

79

INTENTION

"Our intention creates our reality."
– Wayne Dyer

Back in seventh grade, I struggled with Mathematics as a subject. The concepts scared me, and I had a huge fear of failing exams. If we didn't get the answer to a problem the teacher would score it zero out of five marks.

However, soon a progressive system of marking was implemented in schools at that time. According to the approach, even if the final answer to a question was incorrect, the steps that we wrote to solve the Mathematics problem would still count. The teacher would give us step-marking, based on the number of steps we write correctly. So instead of the zero in previous instances, we could now score at least two out of five marks, if our intention to solve was appropriate. The solution might not be accurate, but the intention to answer the question would matter.

> This applies to life too. People observe your actions very keenly. They notice the way you speak to others and even the words you choose to do it. But a major part of your karmic accumulation is your intention too. Whatever you do, the intention of your actions counts.

❖ ❖ ❖ ❖

80

HAPPINESS AND MINDFULNESS

– Mother Teresa

There are so many conversations that revolve around increasing one's happiness quotient and feeling happier. One interesting question is whether you can actually be the happiest you want to be.

Every time we feel happy while spending quality time with friends, or enjoying a family vacation, we are not our happiest. We often ask ourselves how we can be 'happier'. However, in the pursuit of something that doesn't exist, we fail to embrace what we have. Thus, we are not able to take in all the happiness that a particular situation or experience has to offer. That is when the problem begins.

The desire to have more actually nullifies the experience of the present.

This pulls you away from making the best memories, soaking in the moment. This is the power of happiness with mindfulness. You have plenty of moments to feel happy. When you start absorbing each of them to the fullest, that is when you feel happy, while being mindful.

81

INNER PEACE

"Peace comes from within. Do not seek it without."
– Siddhartha Gautama

The traffic on the roads leads to extreme commotion while I drive my car. There is a lot of background noise. Naturally, I increase the volume of the music system in my car as I listen to songs. This automatically nullifies the noise outside the car, which is something I can't really control. But what I can control, is my inner peace, by regulating the volume of the music inside the vehicle.

Similarly, when you are faced with external tensions and pressures, the situations in your outside world cannot be controlled by you. As they increase, they tend to scare you with their burden. What is the solution at that time? All you need to do is raise the volume of your inner voice.

People often feel extremely negative and vulnerable when life challenges them. They feel they can't do anything, and that nothing seems to be in their hands. It is then that they must strengthen their inner practices, lifestyle habits, and consciousness.

This makes sure that even though the extent of your problems and worries in life is too much, your inner peace keeps you strong yet calm. It helps you overcome them with utmost ease while maintaining your sanity.

82

DECLUTTERING EMOTIONS

"Emotions, like a cluttered room, can overwhelm us if left unchecked. Decluttering our surroundings is often the first step to clearing our minds and finding inner peace."
– Sanjay Dua

Have you ever observed a small baby? It only has one emotion to express itself, which is crying. The baby uses this emotion to express practically anything and everything that it wants to. If the baby is hungry, it will cry, if it feels cold, it will cry, and so on. This is because the baby doesn't have a lot of mediums of expression.

However, as the baby grows up into a mature individual, the expression takes different forms. If a person feels happy, they can show that through laughter and can vent out their frustration on feeling angry. The art of using reactions gradually comes with time.

But often, we feel so overwhelmed with all these emotions, that they clutter our mind. You will find that some people's universal expression becomes that of anger. Even when they are in a happy situation, something will end up making them angry. All their output takes the form of anger.

The solution to decluttering your mind is to organise your external world, for example, your messy cupboard. Your output is just a reflection of whatever you feel inside your mind, and vice-versa. If your mind is too cluttered and clumsy, try making your study table tidy, or organise your room. Doing this will help you feel at peace internally, while also keeping everything in order externally.

83

INSECURITIES

– Sanjay Dua

Sometimes, at birthday parties, kids play a fun game where chocolates are put inside a balloon hanging on the ceiling. Kids try to burst the balloon to get the chocolates. I asked a child what the kids would do with so many chocolates. He said they weren't collecting them to eat but to win the game. This small game can teach us so much about insecurities. The kids were collecting the chocolates for a different cause rather than just eating and enjoying them. They wanted to compete and win the game.

As we grow up, we often compete and feel insecure about things like our jobs and relationships. Some people have everything they need, but they're still not happy because they compare themselves to others who seem happier. When you see someone acting this way, it's a sign that they might be going through a tough time.

> But here's the thing; you don't need to be like someone else, and you don't need to make others feel bad. Instead, be true to yourself and work towards becoming the person you want to be. Instead of competing and fighting, focus on being the best version of yourself.

84

BEING PRESENT

Rooh Afza, the name itself brings back so many memories. It is a refreshing drink we enjoyed having during childhood. It contained a red syrup which we used to mix with water.

Some of us would quickly finish the drink, to ensure it doesn't lose its sweetness. However, some kids would sip it very slowly, as they wanted their drink to last longer. They would enjoy two sips, and then again pour water, to raise the level of the drink. Though they would have more to sip in the glass, the Rooh Afza, mixed with too much water, now lost its original taste and sweet flavour. These kids would hold their glasses for a long time, but the drink would have a pale colour, instead of looking bright red.

Life often gives us moments to cherish with friends, family, or any special ones. In such situations, some people enjoy and live those moments to the fullest at that instant itself. While some people choose to save them for later. But this often reduces the originality and magic of those moments.

> The principal idea of mindfulness is to live every moment when it actually takes place. So, celebrate and cherish your special times as and when life presents them to you.

GRATITUDE:
THE FOUNDATION
OF MY JOURNEY

As I reflect on my own journey of growth, learning, and writing, my heart is filled with deep gratitude for the pillars of my life who have shaped my thoughts, encouraged my spirit, and stood by me through every step.

To my parents, your blessings and wisdom have been my guiding light. The values you instilled in me, and the lessons you taught-both spoken and unspoken-have formed the foundation of my thought process. I owe my perspective on life to the love and principles you nurtured in me.

To my wife, my unwavering pillar of strength, thank you for being my constant support, and to my son, who inspires me to become a better version of myself every day. Your patience, love, and encouragement have made all the difference in my journey.

Especially for the journey of writing this book, I wish to thank Ms. Shruti Binani for editing support.

A special thanks to Dinesh Verma and his outstanding team at Pendown Press for their steadfast support and guidance throughout this process.